First I win a contest that
makes me a TV star.
Then I get to do some of
the most awesome extreme
sports in the world. And my
two best friends get
to come along for the ride.
How lucky am I?

First published in Great Britain in 2005 by
RISING STARS UK LTD.
22 Grafton Street, London, W1S 4EX

Reprinted 2007

First published in Australia by Scholastic Australia in 2004.
Text copyright © Philip Kettle, 2004.

A Black Hills book, produced by black dog books

Designed by Blue Boat Design
Cover photo: Blue Boat Design

For more information visit our website at:
www.risingstars-uk.com

British Library Cataloguing in Publication Data

A CIP record for this book is available from the British Library

ISBN 978 1 905056 46 0

Printed in the UK by CPI Bookmarque, Croydon, CR0 4TD

THE XTREME WORLD OF BILLY KOOL

by Phil Kettle

book: 07 kart racing

RISING STARS

CONTENTS

KART RACING EQUIPMENT

Driving Shoes
Driving shoes have special soles that help you grip the accelerator and brake.

Helmet
A special aerodynamic helmet is needed to reduce drag and protect your head in case of an accident.

Racing Tyres
These tyres grip the road like Formula One tyres.

SSC Racing Kart

These karts are like miniature Formula One cars. They go very fast and are low to the ground for fast cornering.

Gloves

Gloves help drivers grip the steering wheel. They are made out of materials such as leather and suede.

Racing Suit

There is the risk you may fall out so you need to protect your body with a full-length racing suit.

MY GRANDAD

On Monday after school, Dad told
me that my grandfather was coming
to stay with us. I was totally rapt.

I hoped for a minute that he might
be coming to live with us, but Dad
said that Grandad was only coming
to stay for a week. Ever since my
grandma died last year, my grandad
has lived on his own. I know that
Grandad sometimes gets lonely. I
guess it must be strange for him
living on his own. My grandad

and grandma had lived together in the same house for fifty years. The house must feel pretty big to him now.

I tried to spend as much time with him as I could. I've always thought of Grandad as more of a friend than just my grandad.

I've always been able to tell him everything—sometimes things that I didn't even tell my parents. Grandad told me that now that he was a grandfather he had the time to be the father that he never was when my dad was young. I kind of knew what he was saying. I loved my dad heaps, but sometimes when I really wanted to do something with him, he was way too busy with his work.

Grandad told me that when he was my dad's age, he was just the same.

'It's really difficult when you're working,' he said. 'Sometimes you have to do work things when you would rather be spending time with your family.'

Grandad helped me understand a lot of things that I had trouble with.

Grandad was really the only person I had ever told that I sometimes thought I wasn't good enough to do the extreme sports we had to do for the show. He told me that if I really wanted to do something then I just had to believe that I could, and I'd be able to.

'Believe in yourself,' he said.
'Chase your dreams. There's a good
chance that they could come true.'

Every time I had doubts about
something I was doing, I thought
about what Grandad had said to me.
That always seemed to make me try
harder.

After every show Grandad would
ring me up to tell me how great the
show was. He was really proud of
what I was doing. He had even rung
Nathan and Sally to tell them how
good they were.

Grandad thought it was fantastic
that I was doing extreme sports.
He always told me that having fun
sometimes meant taking risks. It

was great that Grandad was coming
to stay with us in the week that
our extreme sport was kart racing.
Grandad had built me my first go-
kart.

Not only that, he taught me how to
fish. He even let Nathan come with
us. Nathan thinks Grandad is great,
too.

I really liked going fishing with
Grandad. I liked it more for the
stories that he told when we were
fishing, than the actual fishing itself.
He told me all about the things he
did when he was my age.

Of course, according to Grandad,
everything that he did back then
was better than what we do now. He

called the time when he was young,
the 'olden days'.

When I told Dad about some of
the things that Grandad told me,
Dad said, 'Remember, the older
people get, the better they were.'

I sort of knew what he meant.

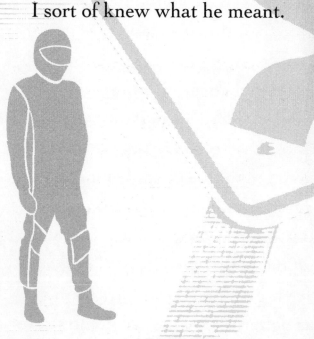

When I got home from school on
Tuesday afternoon, my grandad's
car was parked in the garage.
Grandad had owned the same car
for thirty years. It was his pride and
joy. He must have polished the car
every week. Sometimes I helped
him. There wasn't a single mark on
the car, except for the one near the
front bumper bar. But my grandad
didn't put that ding in his car. I did!

Grandad taught me to drive. I'm

sure my parents would have done
a total flip if they had ever found
out, but Grandad took his car out of
the garage and backed it down the
driveway. He then put two phone
books on the seat and told me to
drive the car to the garage.

We spent all that morning driving
the car thirty metres to the garage
and then reversing it back down the
driveway.

By the end of the morning I was
ready to be a racing car driver. I was
planning a career in Formula One
for when I left school. It was during
the last drive toward the garage that
I must have become too confident.
I must have been going a little too

fast. When I went to put my foot on the brake, I hit the accelerator. The car leapt forward and went straight through the garage doors, knocking them open. I hit the brake, the tyres skidded, and the car pulled up just before the back wall of the garage. The metal rubbish bin that was resting against the back wall was no longer round. It was as flat as a pancake.

Grandad said that was the end of the driving lessons for the day. I thought that he would have been really upset. But he wasn't. He said that sometimes you had to pay a price for learning some things and that a small ding was a small

price. He suggested maybe that we
should keep it our little secret and
not tell my parents about what had
happened. That was fine by me.

THE TALK

Grandad said that he was only going
to stay till after next weekend. He
said that he would have to leave
then so that he could catch the train
home. I asked him why he was
catching the train home and not
driving his car.

He looked at Mum and Dad—he
had a sad look on his face. He said
he wanted to go for a walk and
would I come with him because he
wanted to talk to me.

'I've got something that I want to give you,' Grandad said as he handed me a key.

'What's this for?' I asked.

'This is the key to my car … I mean this is the key to your car,' he said.

'But this is your car,' I said.

'It's your car now,' he said.

'But I'm too young to drive and what are you going to do for a car?'

'You might be too young to drive, but I'm too old to drive,' Grandad said.

I didn't know what to say. Grandad looked smaller than he ever had. His shoulders were hunched and he was walking very slowly.

When we got home, I went into my bedroom and rang Shey. I told her what my grandad had done. Shey said that I should bring Grandad kart racing on the weekend. I really wanted Grandad to know that he wasn't too old. He always told me that you should never give up. I knew that if he gave me his car, he was giving up. I didn't want my grandad to give up.

CAST AND CREW MEETING

On Friday the limo picked us up for the cast and crew meeting. Sally, Nathan and I talked Grandad into coming to the studio. After we'd hassled him for ages, he said that he would come but he still wasn't sure about racing. He said, 'My driving days are over. But when I was younger I think I could have been a champion racing car driver.'

When Nathan asked him why he hadn't become a champion racing car driver, he just smiled and said, 'When I was a boy there wasn't a car invented that was fast enough for me'.

Nathan said that he couldn't wait to race. 'It'll be the first step to becoming a Formula One driver.'

'Well, I hope that you drive a kart better than you ride a mountain bike or you'll never finish the race,' said Sally.

Everyone was really excited to meet Grandad when we got to the meeting. They all shook hands with him. The director said, 'I hope I'm still racing karts when I'm your age, Mr Kool.'

Grandad straightened his

shoulders and asked what he had to do during the filming.

'We'll have kart-cams attached to the karts,' the director said. 'And there'll be two camera crews around the track. You'll all be wired for sound. We'll have all the safety equipment ready for you when you get to the track tomorrow. So all you have to do, Mr Kool, is try to beat these kids around the track.'

'I think I can do that,' Grandad said.

'This will be a great episode,' the director said. 'The limo will pick you up at nine tomorrow.'

Location Map

1. Starting grid
2. Old tyres to stop you skidding off the road
3. Hairpin—sharp corner
4. Main stretch
5. Pit lane
6. Sound crew based for monitoring

Our Equipment

SSC Racing Kart

Gloves

Driving Shoes

Helmet

Racing Tyres

Racing Suit

LIGHTS,
CAMERA, ACTION

BILLY
Hi and welcome to *The Xtreme World Of Billy Kool*. My name is Billy Kool and as usual my co-hosts Nathan and Sally are with me. Today we are standing at the racing track. Our extreme sport today is kart racing.

NATHAN
Hi, Billy, and viewers. It's great to be here today. I can't wait to get on the track and burn some rubber.

SALLY
Good morning, everyone. And good morning to you, Nathan and Billy.

BILLY
Kart racing is one of the
best adrenaline sports
you can do. Did you know
that most of the world's
Formula One racing drivers
started by racing karts?

NATHAN
That's why I think
that if there's a
Formula One racing team
watching,they'll offer me
a contract after today.

SALLY
Yeah, right, whatever.

BILLY
As usual, our safety co-
ordinator, Shey, is also
with us. Before we started
filming today's show, we
did some practice laps of

the racetrack. Shey was
really good.

SHEY
Thank you, Billy. Today
is really special for
me. Kart racing is my
favourite extreme sport.
The best thing about
extreme kart racing is
that you get to go so fast
and are so close to the
ground.

BILLY
Today is really special
for me too. I would like
to introduce my grandad.
Grandad is going to prove
to everyone that extreme
sports can be enjoyed by
people of all ages.

GRANDAD walks to where BILLY, NATHAN, SALLY and SHEY are standing. He is wearing a driving suit and looks nervous and excited.

GRANDAD
Where do I stand and where do I look?

BILLY
Just stand next to me and look at the camera!

Grandad smiles at the camera.

SHEY
So, Mr Kool, do you think that you'll be the fastest around the track?

GRANDAD
I'm not too sure about

that. I just hope that
I get around the track
without having an
accident.

BILLY
I reckon that you'll
probably be the fastest
and best driver—after me
of course.

SHEY
It's time to get into our
karts and find out how
good we are.

BILLY
The karts that we are
using are special SSC
racing karts.

SALLY
And what does SSC
stand for?

BILLY
I have no idea.

NATHAN
I think it means that the karts can go really fast!

SHEY
When we're racing, it's good to wear protective clothing.

SALLY
As you can see we have driving suits on.

BILLY
We're also wearing helmets.

NATHAN
We're also wearing gloves that will help us hold the steering wheel. Kart racing can get bumpy.

GRANDAD
We've also got special
shoes on. We all look like
we've just come from outer
space.

SHEY
We're going to race for
four laps. First person
over the finishing line
wins. It's time to get
into our karts and start
the engines.

*Grandad, Shey, Sally,
Nathan and Billy get into
their karts and start the
engines. The karts move
toward the starting line.
The starting marshal
moves into position and
prepares to wave the
chequered flag.*

BILLY
This is how it must feel
for the drivers in Formula
One racing when they line
up on the grid.

NATHAN
I feel like I'm about to
travel at the speed of
light.

SALLY
When both of you have
crashed into the edge of
the track, I'll still be
going around the track. So
will Grandad.

GRANDAD
I'm not too sure about
this, Billy.

*The starter raises the
flag above his head.*

The motors of the karts scream. The starter brings the flag down. The race begins. The karts race off from the starting line.

BILLY
This is the first of the four laps. I'm in front, but Nathan's close behind me.

NATHAN
All our karts have exactly the same engine size.

SALLY
That means that the winner will be the driver that has the best skills.

The karts go down the straight. Billy first, Nathan second, Sally

*third, Shey fourth,
Grandad fifth. Grandad is
gaining on Shey.*

GRANDAD
These karts are really
flying.

NATHAN
It feels as if I'm
travelling at a million
kilometres per hour.

BILLY
That's because the karts
are so close to the
ground! Are you having a
good time, Grandad?

GRANDAD
I should have done this
years ago.

Nathan and Billy get

*through the first corner
without mishap. They zoom
off.*

SALLY
Watch out, I'm going into
the corner.

SHEY
So am I. Make sure you
leave enough room for me.

*Shey and Sally's karts
reach the corner at the
same time. Grandad is
close behind.*

*Sally hasn't slowed enough
to take the corner.
Her kart goes straight
through the corner and
crashes into the old
tyres that line the edge
of the track. She heads*

*off Shey's kart and Shey
is forced to drive into
the old tyres as well.
Grandad makes it through
and sets off after Billy
and Nathan.*

SALLY
Sorry, Shey. I just lost
it. I didn't slow down
enough to go into the
corner. I've lost a lot of
ground. But I'm going to
try and come back.

SHEY
No worries. All's fair in
love and kart racing!

*Sally and Shey manoeuvre
their karts out of the
tyre barrier and begin
driving again. Billy and
Nathan have completed*

their first lap. Grandad is right on their tails as Billy goes into a corner.

BILLY
My back wheels are slipping and sliding. This is where you really test your skills as a driver. Look out! I'm doing a massive spin out.

Billy's kart starts to spin. The back end of the kart slides around—the kart is now facing the oncoming karts. Nathan reaches the corner at the same time as Billy.

NATHAN
Get out of the way! I'm going to crash straight into you, Billy.

CRASH! The two karts collide. Grandad goes wide and races past them.

GRANDAD
See you later, boys. Now it's time for me to show you all how a good driver races their kart.

BILLY
Go Grandad! Lucky we've got all the right safety gear on, Nathan.

NATHAN
Yeah, that's for sure.

Sally and Shey catch up to Billy and Nathan and pass them.

NATHAN
We are so far behind.

Billy
Don't worry about me – I'm
making a comeback.

SHEY
These karts have got more
power than you think and
it takes a lot of skill to
drive them.

SALLY
I thought it would be like
racing dodgem cars.

*Billy and Nathan get their
karts going again. Nathan
races into a corner. Again
his kart spins out of
control and he comes to a
stop.*

GRANDAD
You can't put your foot
on the brake when you're

in the corner or you will lose control.

BILLY
I knew you'd be the best driver, Grandad.

Grandad is well in front. Shey is coming second, with Sally close behind her. Billy is half a lap behind them, and Nathan is a full lap behind them.

SALLY
This is awesome. I really feel like a racing driver.

GRANDAD
I haven't had so much fun since…well I can't remember when I have ever had as much fun.

SHEY
You're nearly at the
finishing line, Mr Kool.

GRANDAD
I've passed it!

BILLY
You won, Grandad! That
just proves that you're
still a great driver.

GRANDAD
Well, maybe I can still
drive for a few more years
yet.

BILLY/NATHAN/SALLY/SHEY
Of course you can!

NATHAN
Now we're racing for
second place. May the
second-best driver win!

Sally and Shey are head-to-head as they race down the final straight. It's impossible to tell who's in front.

SALLY
Ahhhhhhhhh! This is awesome.

GRANDAD
It's a photo finish!

Sally's kart crosses the line a few centimetres in front of Shey's.

SHEY
Good race, Sally!

SALLY
Hurry up, Billy and Nathan. Let's go again.

Billy overtakes Nathan on

the straight and crosses the finishing line.

NATHAN
No way did I come last. We have to race again.

Billy drives his kart into the pit lane. He gets out of the kart and takes his helmet off.

BILLY
While the others do a few practice laps, it's time for me to wind up the show. Maybe Grandad will be able to give Nathan and me a few tips on how to take the corners.

I've had the best time racing karts. I'm sure that I will soon be back here racing again. On behalf of Nathan, Sally and all the crew, thank you for watching our show. Remember, extreme sports are the real thing. My name is Billy Kool. See you soon.

DIRECTOR
Cut! Well done. That was a great show. Now one of you bring your kart into the pit. I want to have a drive.

BILLY
I've got to get back out on the track. I reckon that I'm a better driver

than they are—now I just
have to prove it.

GRANDAD
Hurry up, Billy, and
get back out onto the
track. Fancy letting your
grandfather beat you.

BILLY
Well, we'll just have to
see about that.

NATHAN
This is awesome. I'm
finally getting the hang
of the corners. Oh-oh! No
I'm not.

SALLY
None of you are as good as
me.

EVERYONE
Yeah, right.

DIRECTOR
Okay, Shey, bring your
kart in. I want to have a
go.

SHEY
What was that? I can't
hear you above the noise
of the engines. It's so
loud out here.

DIRECTOR
I said, bring your kart
in. I want a go.

SHEY
Sorry. I have no idea what
you just said.

DIRECTOR
Billy? Sally? Nathan? Mr
Kool?

EVERYONE
What was that?

DIRECTOR
I said…oh just forget it.
You're all acting like
you're six years old. Even
you, Mr Kool.

THE WRAP UP

I'm glad that my grandad taught me
to drive. With a bit more practise
I'm sure I could end up being a
Formula One driver.

Nathan reckons that he's better
than me. But he has to learn how to
go around corners a lot better than
he did.

Grandad's decided that he is still
able to drive his car. That's really
good! He told me that during the
next holidays we might go for a big

road trip. Grandad told me that the car is still mine, but he wants to drive it for a while yet. By the time he's really ready to stop driving it, I'll be ready to start. My grandad is really cool!

Dear Billy

Do you think that you will be doing more shows next year? If you don't, I will be really upset!

Can you send me a signed picture of you with Nathan and Sally?

Caitlin, one of your biggest fans

Extreme Information
History

Since the invention of the first go-kart in 1956, kart racing has become more and more popular all over the world.

One of the biggest reasons for this is that people of all different ages can get involved in go-karting (or karting as the professionals like to call it). There are licensed drivers from ages seven to seventy. There are also karting centres, with special tracks built just for go-karts, in most capital cities. They provide the karts, racing equipment and safety gear for anyone wanting to have a go.

Karting is also an internationally

recognised sport and is highly competitive. Many of the world's greatest Formula One drivers, such as Nigel Mansell and Alain Prost, began their careers kart racing. They perfected their skills kart racing before moving onto other motorsports.

Karting is also a much cheaper motorsport than Formula One.

There are different categories of go-kart too. The first is known as the Super Kart. These karts actually race on the race-car circuits used by Formula One. Super karts have a big engine and can travel at speeds up to 260 kilometres per hour. They even have a gear box, just like a car.

The second type of kart is a Sprint Kart. They have a smaller engine than the

Super Kart and have no gears. They race on tracks built especially for them which are usually no longer than a kilometre long. They are narrower than race-car tracks which means they race a lot closer to one another, making for a very exciting race.

Glossary

Apex
Point where the kart is turning the most sharply.

Back marker
A kart that is running near the back of the field.

Binding
A term used to describe the kart slowing down excessively in the turns because both rear tyres are planted too firmly on the ground.

Blistering
When racing tyres overheat.

Disqualification
A severe punishment when racing

for ignoring flags, breaking rules or deliberately damaging another kart.

Flags

Flags are used to communicate with drivers.

—Green flag

The signal to start.

—Black flag

A black flag means the driver must report to the pit immediately.

—Yellow flag

Slow down/danger ahead.

—Blue flag with diagonal yellow

A blue flag with diagonal yellow means that a faster car is approaching or someone is following close.

—Black and white chequered flag

Signals the end of race.

Grid

Grid is short for starting grid. This is the order in which the drivers line up for the race start. This order is usually determined through qualifying heats.

Hairpin

Sharp 180° turn.

Horsepower

The power of the engine is measured in horsepower.

Oversteering

When the kart enters a corner, the rear tyres lose grip before the front tyres, and the rear of the kart slides towards the outside of the curve. This is called 'oversteering'.

Pits

Area where the kart is taken to refuel,
change tyres and be repaired.

Shunt

A crash/accident.

Equipment

Clothes

Kart drivers are required to wear purpose-made and approved driving suits or leathers, approved safety helmets, gloves and lace-up shoes that cover the ankles.

Karts

Karts are state-of-the-art driving machines, which are about two metres long and 1.2 metres wide, with a base height from the ground of about ten centimetres. They weigh around 100 kilograms and come fitted with auto-transmission gears. They usually have 180cc engines. Depending on the length of the track, these karts could be accelerated to speeds up to 100 kilometres per hour. Considering their low base heights and maximum speeds at this level, kart racing is pretty extreme.

Karts are designed to protect the driver.

Specially built tyre barriers around the circuit protect the driver from injury, should they veer off the track.

PHIL KETTLE

Phil Kettle lives in inner-city Melbourne, Australia. He has three children, Joel, Ryan and Shey. Originally from northern Victoria, Phil grew up on a vineyard. He played football and cricket and loved any sport where he could kick, hit or throw something.

These days, Phil likes to go to the Melbourne Cricket Ground on a winter afternoon and cheer on his favourite Australian Rules team, the Richmond Tigers. Phil hopes that one day he will be able to watch the Tigers win a grand final—'Even if that means I have to live till I'm 100.'

THE Xtreme WORLD OF BILLY KOOL

by Phil Kettle

Billy Kool books are available
from most booksellers.
For mail order information
please call Rising Stars on
0870 40 20 40 8 or visit
www.risingstars-uk.com